Mini House Now

First Edition
published in 2006 by:
Collins Design
An Imprint of HarperCollins*Publishers*
10 East 53rd Street
New York, NY 10022
Tel.: (212) 207-7000
Fax: (212) 207-7654
Collinsdesign@harpercollins.com
www.harpercollins.com

Distributed throughout the world by:
HarperCollins*Publishers*
10 East 53rd Street
New York, NY 10022
Fax: (212) 207-7654

Packaged by:
LOFT Publications
Via Laietana, 32 4.° Of. 92
08003 Barcelona, Spain
Tel.: +34 932 688 088
Fax: +34 932 687 073
loft@loftpublications.com
www.loftpublications.com

Editor:
Àgata Losantos

Translation:
Jay Noden

Art Director:
Mireia Casanovas Soley

Layout:
Zahira Rodríguez Mediavilla

Library of Congress Cataloging-in-Publication Data

Losantos, Agata.
  Mini house now / Agata Losantos. —1st ed.
     p. cm.
  ISBN-13: 978-0-06-113933-8 (hardcover)
  ISBN-10: 0-06-113933-5 (hardcover)
1. Small houses. 2. Architect-designed houses. I. Title.
  NA7533.L67 2006
  728'.37—dc22
                                    2006015633

Printed in Spain

First Printing, 2006

Mini House Now

Àgata Losantos

COLLINS|DESIGN

An Imprint of HarperCollinsPublishers

introduction

There could be a multitude of reasons for creating a small home. The most common however are; a limited budget, the surface area of the site and the seasonal or ephemeral use of the building. The architect must take these reasons into account, finding ingenious solutions which allow the house, no matter how small it is, to provide the occupants with all the basic needs: to rest, eat, work and wash.

The projects in *Mini House Now* are all below 120 square yards and situated in highly diverse locations. Needless to say the positioning of mini houses generates very different typologies of construction: while in a rural environment opening up the house blurs boundaries, the proximity of the neighbors in an urban setting requires other resources to visually amplify the available surface area. Likewise a harsh or pleasant climate means the use of more or less resources, time and square yards to achieve good insulation, which will make a large difference to the final result.

The use of the construction is another fundamental factor when designing such challenging projects. Making the most out of every square inch, a basic requirement in any home, is often not the case in a summerhouse where priority is given to larger living areas or the creation of an outdoor space. On the other hand, in a mini house built as an annex to a main building, functions such as rest or other auxiliary functions dominate the design, so again the layout here is not typical.

Structurally speaking, mini houses often share certain features, which can be identified in the projects presented in this book. Small often goes hand in hand with simple, open and orthogonal: these characteristics help optimize the use of space and lower costs. The absence of divisions and a choice of furniture that can be easily converted or moved, guarantees the creation of versatile and seemingly large rooms, two key elements when dealing with small dimensions. Also, technological advances, which have reduced the sizes of various household objects, to incredible degrees in some cases, are great allies to architects, not only regarding furniture, lighting and domestic appliances, but also concerning materials and constructive solutions.

Mini House Now brings together more than twenty homes with diverse locations, surface areas and functions, providing a thorough sample of the architectural resources used today to reduce the home to its essence, maximizing the efficiency of minimal spaces.

Photos © Sascha Kletzsch

Micro-Compact Home

H. Cherry Lee Architects & L. Haack, J. Höpfner Architekten Germany

Micro-Compact Home—or M-ch, for short—was developed from the i-home project, a light 8.5-foot cube commissioned by the Studentenwerk of Munich. In terms of space usage, M-ch draws on aeronautical and automobile design, while its scale and harmonies come from the architecture of the classic Japanese teahouse. Within its space of under 75-square-feet, this cube offers a space for each of the four basic requirements of a home: to rest, work, eat, and wash. Inside this wooden and aluminum structure, the foldaway bed can be found above the rest of the space. The work area can be converted into another bed. The kitchen is perfectly equipped and includes two work areas, one at the height of the "bedroom" and another at the height of the dining room. The bathroom is situated next to the hallway, which also provides a space to dry laundry. M-ch is manufactured in just one production center in Austria, and from there it is distributed throughout Europe. M-ch offers the option of choosing the exterior appearance and interior finishes, and can be installed in a garden as a single unit for private use or joined with other volumes to create a small community, such as a student residence or accommodation for tourists.

Munich played host to the first M-ch student residence, sponsored by O_2, a German telecommunications company.

Micro-Compact Home rises from the ground via a light aluminum structure that also provides terrace space.

All that is superfluous has been eliminated from Micro-Compact Home's interior, reducing the house to its essence.

In the M-ch project, various environmental criteria were taken into account, such as reducing energy consumption, ensuring good insulation, and using an air-conditioning and heating system is easy to use and adjust.

M-ch is equipped with a built-in sound system, as well as two flat-screen television sets and a broadband Internet connection.

A large storage space hides beneath the seats in the dining and work area.

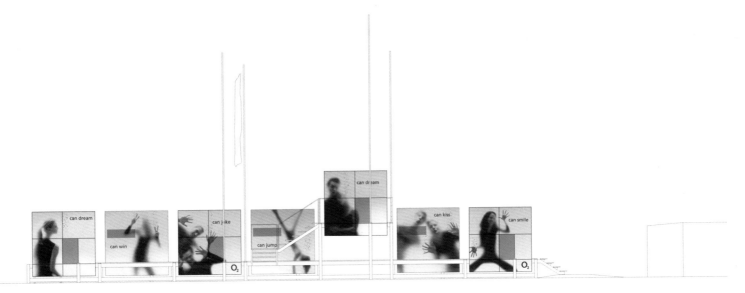

Village elevation

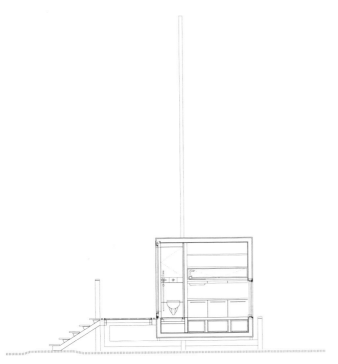

Cross section

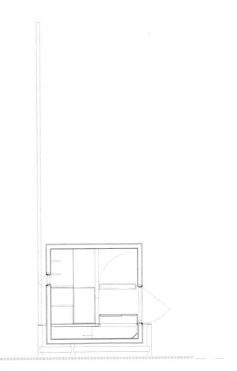

Longitudinal section

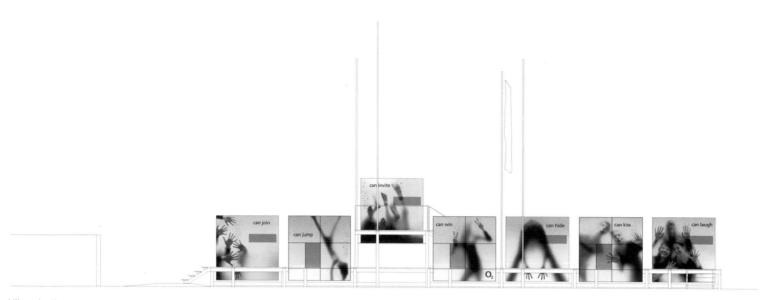

Village elevation

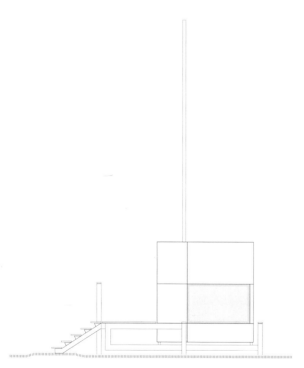

Elevation

Floor plan

Photos © Ben Rahn/A-Frame

Sunset Cabin

Taylor Smyth Architects Lake Simcoe, Canada

Due to the wave of visitors who occupy the house throughout the summer, the owners of Sunset Cabin commissioned architects to design a small cabin that could be used to escape the chaos in the main house. The clients laid down one basic condition: that they would be able to see the sunset from the bed. For four weeks, a group of carpenters adjusted and assembled every piece of the volume in a car lot in Toronto, before numbering, dismantling, and later reassembling them on the site in just 10 days. Sunset Cabin sits on a wooden platform that extends past the cabin like a terrace and is used for the outdoor shower. Cedar paneling

protects the shower from the sun, hiding both the shower and the interior of the house from sight since three of the four walls are made of glass. The distance between the panels increases in certain random points, giving the cabin's occupants an almost abstract composition of sky, vegetation, and water. Likewise, as requested by the clients, the large opening in the wall in front of the bed allows the viewing of the sunset from inside the house. Given the spectacular setting of the house, Sunset Cabin's 275-square-foot area could be defined more as a large viewing gallery with an adjoining bedroom than as a mini house with a terrace.

Since the roof of the cabin was visible from the main house, the architects opted to cover it in vegetation in order to integrate it with the environment.

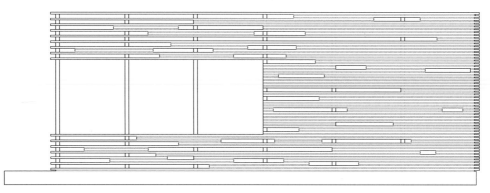

West elevation

As the evening advances, the sun, which filters through the openings in the façade, creates a changing pattern of light and shade in the home's interior.

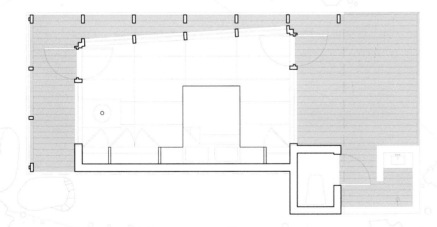

Floor plan

Photos © Romain Machefer

Catherine House

Andy Macdonald/Mac-Interactive Architecture   Leichhardt, Australia

Catherine House is situated in Leichhardt, an area known as Little Italy in Sydney. The project was based on the reconversion and extension of a simple house built in the 1950's, formed from a single floor that included a living room that looked onto the street, followed by a bedroom, and then finally a bathroom. In 1985, the first renovation added a kitchen, taking up space from the back garden. Andy MacDonald designed a completely different home of 990-square-feet inverting the original layout: the living room and bedroom changed places. These two rooms were divided by stairs that ascended to the new first floor, used for

the main bedroom and a terrace. Given the proximity of the neighboring houses, special attention was paid to avoid blocking either the sunlight or the views of the adjoining buildings. Also, bearing in mind that the clients' basic requisite was to respect the environment in all aspects of the renovation, the architect used recycled and sustainable materials; built a rainwater collector whose contents could be used in the bathroom and kitchen; provided shade for the east façade with a screen of mobile wooden paneling; and achieved an effective cross-ventilation system, which made the installation of air-conditioning unnecessary.

The positioning of the openings on the first floor was carefully studied to reduce the possibility of seeing inside and to maximize the cross-ventilation.

Following the environmental criteria applied throughout the renovation, a system for heating the water using solar energy was installed in the roof.

Longitudinal section

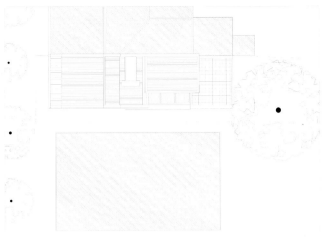

Roof plan

First-floor plan

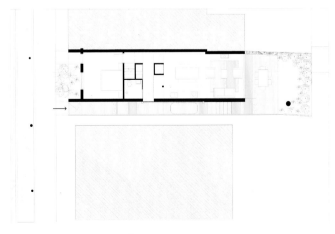

Ground-floor plan

The slope of the plot allowed the division of the ground floor spaces using the changing level, lowering the living room to the same height as the back yard.

The renovation allowed for the extension of the house by almost 315-square-feet, and opened the living area to the yard.

Practically all of the materials obtained from the demolition of the original house were used in the construction of the new one.

Photos © Johannes Felsch, Caramel

Kaps House

Caramel Architekten Saalfelden am Steineren Meer, Austria

The name Kaps House comes from its similarity in shape and function to a space capsule. Kaps House needs the mother ship—i.e. the existing house—, but constitutes a completely independent space. Conceived as an extension of a country house dating back to the 13th century, Kaps House has its own entrance, although it can also be accessed via the main house. Despite its modern, rounded shape, the new construction interacts well with the neighboring building, whose traditional appearance is reinforced. Kaps House is formed from two same sized volumes that are joined by a hallway. The roof, which in total hardly exceeds 540-square-feet, is built as a terrace, which can be accessed from a stairway situated in the corridor that separates the original house from the extension. The two volumes are covered in fiberglass and PVC, except on the east and west façades, which open to the splendid alpine landscape through large windows. The east-facing construction is reserved for the bedroom and bathroom, while the living room and kitchen share the other volume.

A light metal staircase gives access to the extension without the need to pass through the main house.

The materials and structure of Kaps House form a strong contrast with the traditional wooden cladding and morphology of the original house.

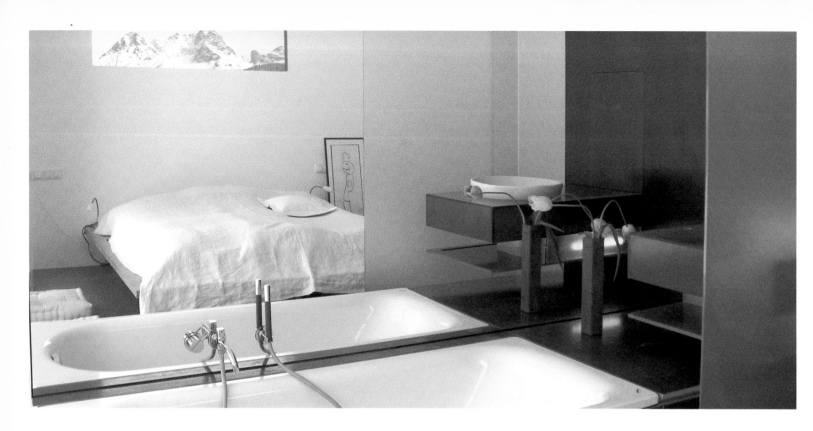

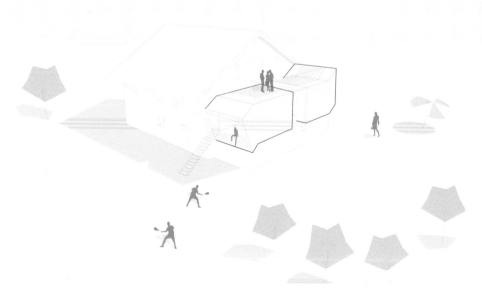

Perspective

At the eastern end of Kaps House, the roof slopes towards the floor, while at the western end it rises, exposing the house to the setting sun. This special roof also gives the space a feeling of movement.

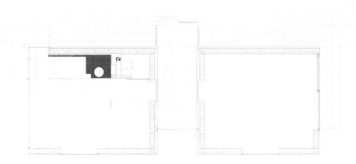

Floor plan

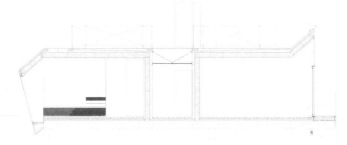

Longitudinal section

The notable contrast in materials and lines between the original construction and the enlargement add value to the whole.

The absence of divisions and the large windows on the eastern and western sides make up for the shortage of square metres.

Photos © Eightyseven

Summer Garden Pavilion

Artur Carulla, Rita Lambert/Eightyseven   Sant Miquel de Cruïlles, Spain

Sant Miquel de Cruïlles is a small village in the northeast of Catalonia, situated just a few miles from the French border. The place is especially known for its Romanic monastery, around which the village has grown, and is formed today by no more than 10 houses. The owners of these houses commissioned Eightyseven with the construction of a small volume that was to be used as a guesthouse in the summer and as storage space in the winter. Through a system of sliding and folding doors and windows, this compact Corten stainless steel volume becomes a mini home open to the yard in warmer months. Its morphology is characterized by a fragmented geometry, which invites the onlooker to walk around the perimeter, enjoying the surprises provided by each façade. The two triangular skylights, arranged on different planes of the asymmetric cube, combine to create this discontinuous structure. The coarse Corten cladding, chosen for its durability and its similarity to the roofs of neighboring houses, contrasts in the interior with the flooring and the walls, which use an extremely resistant wood of Brazilian origin.

The bareness of this garden pavilion, where the only permanent feature is the kitchen furniture, makes this an extremely versatile space.

From the inside, the openings frame particular points of the rural surroundings, which stretch beyond the garden.

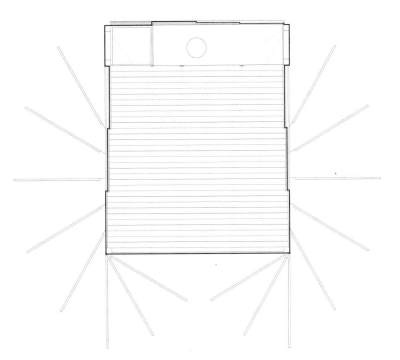

Floor plan

B House

Atelier A5   Tokyo, Japan

B House is situated in a densely populated residential area of Tokyo. A house capable of accommodating two generations of a family had to be built on this 755-square-foot site, providing everyone with their own private space and including a meeting point. Also, given the proximity of the neighbors, a solution had to be found to make the best use of the available surface area without sacrificing the occupants' sense of intimacy. One space was used for each generation, vertically distributing the house's 875-square-feet, with the ground floor housing the communal area, including the living room and kitchen. In terms of space

usage, and the search for privacy, the project attempted to distance the building from the neighbors by creating an empty space around the house, delimited by metal translucent netting that follows the boundaries of the plot. In the living room, the sliding windows can be taken out completely to extend the usable surface area, thanks to the terrace with its metal railings. In keeping with the closed-open-closed alternation and with the desire to differentiate between the areas destined for different generations, the upper floor is a parallelepiped clad in metal, which breaks with the rest of the building's aesthetics from the outside.

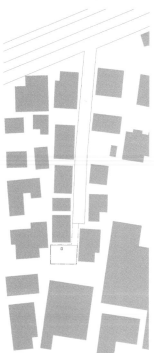

Location plan

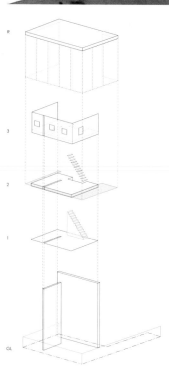

Exploded view

Two earthquake-resistant concrete walls constitute the heart of the house, since their role both in the structure and in the division of spaces is fundamental on all floors.

With the exception of the two reinforcing walls, the structure is made from wood, guaranteeing a reduction in the construction time and costs.

Ground-floor plan

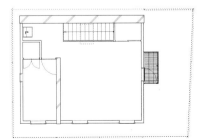

First-floor plan

Second-floor plan

Photos © Joseph Pettyjohn

Lake House

Bercy Chen Studio Lago Vista, United States

This weekend home is situated on the banks of Lake Travis, in the magnificent hill country of Texas. In contrast with the arid image often associated with this state, the environment of Lake House is characterized by changing scenery and a wide variety of fauna to which the architects have opened the house. To achieve this, they designed a simple house of 880-square-feet formed from oblique planes—base and roof—that delimit a wooden and glass volume. Due to the simplicity of the lines and materials, Lake House resembles a delicate Japanese garden pavilion, immersed in the rugged Texan countryside. The concrete base, raised above the plot, supports a volume of large windows framed by a steel structure. While the entrance façade, clad in wood, is totally opaque, the other walls open to the panorama of the cedar forest that surrounds the home. The roof, which slopes steeply, juts far past the volume and protects the large porch. Inside, the polished cement flooring contrasts with the wood of the walls and ceiling. The living room, kitchen, and bedroom share a single space, while the only interior wall hides the bathroom.

The combination of wood and glass allows the house to integrate perfectly with the forested surroundings.

Thanks to the slope of the roof, the house makes full use of the hours of sunshine.

OUTDOOR PATIO

BEDROOM

SUNKEN FIRE PIT

LIVING / DINING

BATH

ENTRY

KITCHEN

Floor plan

The almost complete absence of partitions in the interior allows the numerous visitors to the house to adapt the space to their needs.

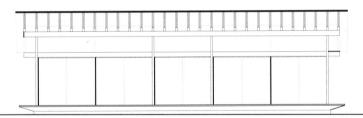

South elevation

The continuity of the polished cement floor and the large openings on the southern perimeter blur the line between the interior and exterior.

This home's reduced dimensions allow it to be heated by one sunken pit located in the middle of the main room.

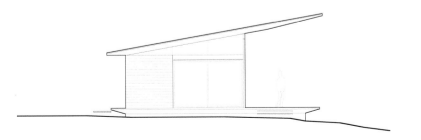

East elevation

Photos © Paul Ott, Graz

Uncle Fred's Hut

Hertl Architekten   Steyr, Austria

The architects were commissioned with designing a two-person home with a very restricted budget. Given that the town planning regulations in the area put strict limits on the surface area available for construction, Hertl had to find numerous pragmatic solutions to maximize the sense of size in just 477-square-feet. Despite the limited surface area, the volume, which is clearly different from the traditional architecture in the area, fulfills all of the requisites specified by the client. With a large part of the perimeter clad in fir wood, only the living room on the ground floor opens completely to the exterior via French windows. Due to the appearance of the house's solid volume, the windows, slightly set back with respect to the façade, seem like blocks of wood extracted from the building. To allow sufficient height for the two floors, a hole was dug 7 feet into the plot. Stairs descend to the level of the entrance and down to the porch situated in front of the window to the living room. The living area is on the ground floor, while the upper floor is reserved for the bedroom and study. The stairs separate the kitchen from the living room downstairs, and the study from the bed and bath upstairs, which—due to the changing level—are at the same height as the ground.

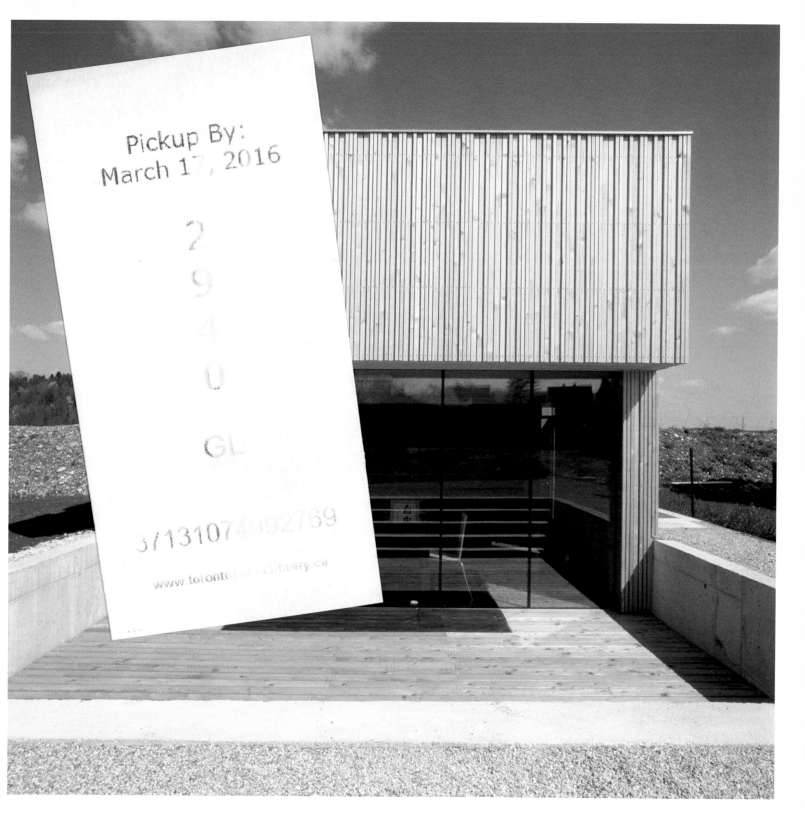

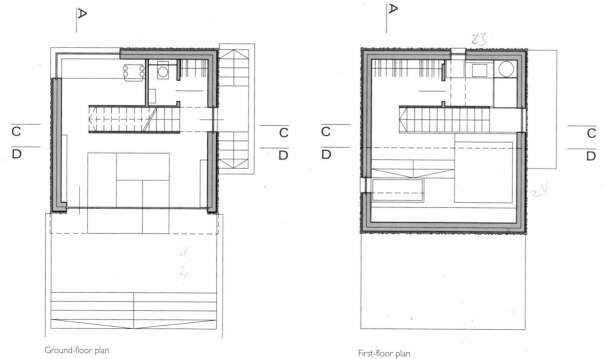

The dining area is reflective of traditional Japanese architecture, since it is structured on the base of the rectangular tatami and delimited by a change in color of the floor.

The window of the living room is set back, compared with the rest of the façade, gaining space for the terrace and avoiding too much sun in the bedroom.

Ground-floor plan

First-floor plan

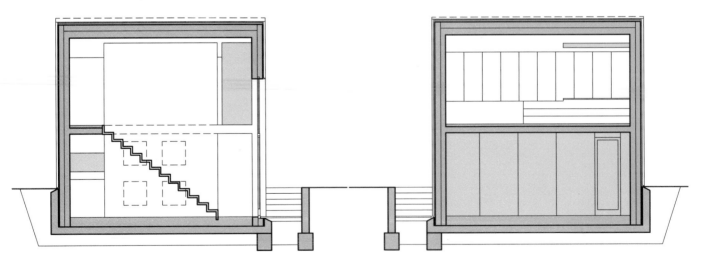

Cross sections

All of the interior of the house is clad in varnished chipboard, which is darker in certain areas to distinguish the different rooms.

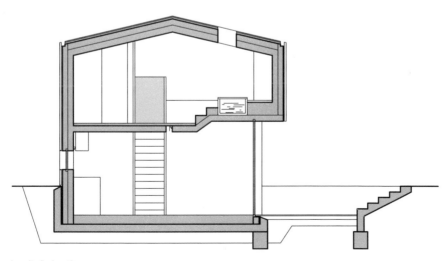

Longitudinal section

C-2 House

Curiosity Yamanashi, Japan

Yamanashi is a prefecture of the island of Honshu, known mainly for the world- famous Mount Fuji, indisputable star of the typical Japanese postcard. C-2 House sits in this mountainous scenery and, according to the architects, enhances the beauty of the surrounding nature. A wooden walkway crosses through the house and ends at the terrace, where the panorama is spectacular. From the north, the 300-square-foot volume looks like a half-buried mountain home; and from the south, C-2 appears more as a square, two-story, minimalist block. On the ground floor, which can be accessed from the walkway or from the opposite façade, a single

space with different levels and a maximum height of 20 feet plays host to the living room, dining room and kitchen, which extend toward the forest via a terrace. The careful arrangement of the windows and of the points of indirect light generates a constantly changing interior, thanks largely to the intense chromatic contrast between the floor, walls and ceiling. The sleeping area is situated in the basement, set into the changing level of the plot. The bedrooms and bathroom are arranged parallel to the longitudinal axis, receive an abundance of natural light and have a direct access to the exterior.

The light-dark-light alternation in the access tunnel corresponds to the architect's desire to leave the visitor speechless before the spectacular scenery.

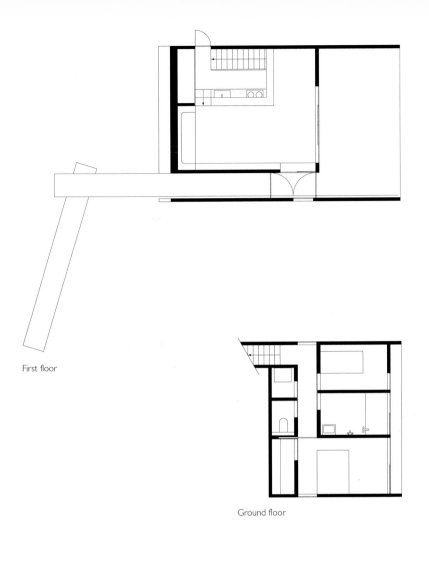

First floor

Ground floor

When the land around C-2 House is covered in snow, nature seems to enter the house through the bathroom window, where the whiteness continues without interruption.

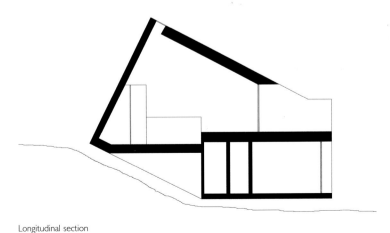

Longitudinal section

Photos © Kei Sugino

Window House

Kentaro Takeguchi/Alphaville   Kyoto, Japan

With great ingenuity, the Japanese Alphaville solved the difficult challenge of constructing a home of nearly 855-square-feet on an extremely narrow site of 558-square-feet. Window House's solemn metallic volume stands out from the surrounding heterogeneous residential area, which is typical of the network of alleyways in any large Japanese city. Large windows, which take up the 25-foot high facades at the northeast and southeast corners of this rectangular blck, open the building to the outside, which features two triangular courtyards. Due to the original layout of the spaces, the two openings can be seen from any point inside the home. Because of the absence of doors, the different levels have been used to separate the rooms. These join at the central section of the building, where the three flights of the stylized sheet metal staircase converge. The ground floor, the only part to occupy the 315-square-foot surface area, encompasses the kitchen, dining room, and bathroom. The first flight of stairs ascends to the living room, and the two remaining floors, arranged on opposing sides of the central axis, house the dressing room and bedroom. Each of these three floors comprise 162-square-feet.

The cold colors and materials, as well as the complete sparseness of the spaces, generate the extreme minimalism of this home.

Window House's peculiar structure is especially evident in the top floor, where part of the building's steel structure remains visible.

With the aim of optimizing the building's height of 25 feet, three floors measuring only 162-square-feet each were set at different levels.

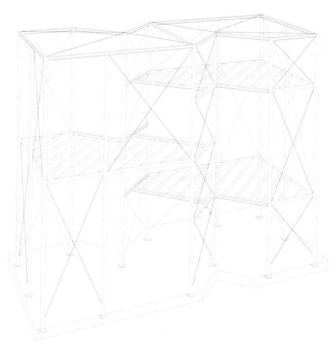

Axonometric view

Photos © Peter Bennetts

Nobbs Radford Architects   Dulwich Hill, Sydney, Australia

The original 965-square-foot house was a typical construction of Sydney's residential neighborhoods, situated at the end of the street. An extension added 935-square-feet of usable surface area, distributed in a single-story volume annexed to the existing home. The renovation started with the specification of new communal and private areas: was reserved the original construction for the bedrooms, while the extension housed the kitchen, dining room, and living room, as well as a bedroom with an extra bathroom. A brick path cuts through the house and joins the entrance with the back yard. This path is the fruit of the reorganization of

the space that separates the two volumes from the street; something which had not been dealt with until the changes. The reorganization also implied the creation of a new courtyard in the entrance, to which the extension opens by way of the practicable lattice in the dining and living rooms. A series of elements were distributed along the street side to mark the alternation between open and closed, public and private, transparent and opaque. The architects not only achieved their objective of reinterpreting the context of the residential neighborhood, but also provided a new space that met the clients' needs.

The front yard is the transition area between the public and private space, delimited by the front-facing visuals: a small pond running parallel to the front door.

The latticed walls guarantee optimum cross-ventilation throughout the volume.

The coldness of the polished cement and aluminum structure is counteracted by the explosion of colors in the brick floor and in the built-in cupboards that stretch from wall to wall.

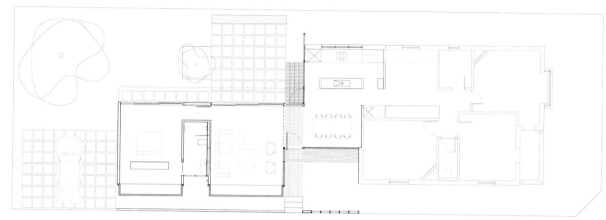

Floor plan

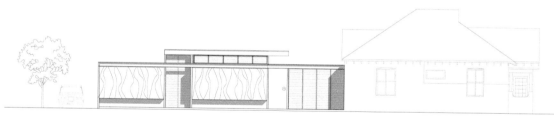

South elevation

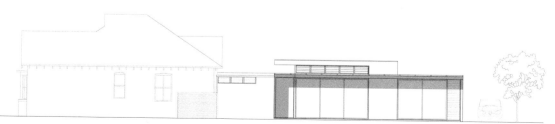

North elevation

The austerity of the straight lines in the new volume, together with the careful alternation between accessible and private spaces, contrasts with the innocuouss neighboring constructions, which are identical to those in any other suburban residential area in a big city.

Photos © Ester Hazlova

A House in the Garden

Archteam   Kromeriz, Czech Republic

Kromeriz is a medium-sized city with a rich historical and architectural heritage, situated in the fertile plains of Moravia. This 90-square-foot house sits on an elongated and considerably narrow plot on the outskirts of the city center, and has been defined by architects as an item of garden furniture. The bizarre dimensions of the plot determined the morphology of the building, a parallelepiped delimited by two nearly opaque façades and two others that open to the garden through large French windows. The external symmetry of this wooden and glass volume is interrupted only by a wooden structure that juts out from the upper story and marks the access to the home.

The interior is composed of a ground floor without partitions, except for the hall, and an upper floor, where only the bathroom has been separated via glass walls. The wooden furniture, distributed strategically throughout the two floors in order to suggest different rooms, provides the only visible barriers. The ground floor is used as a livingroom and kitchen, while the first floor plays host to the bedroom and bathroom, overlooking the living area. The entrance porch is located on the terrace of the first floor, which stretches toward the outside on a suspended wooden structure.

While wood dominates both the external and the internal structure, sheets of zinc and titanium were used for the lightly sloping gable roof.

A light and simple single-flight wooden staircase gives access to the first floor.

The ample presence of glass in the house and the practical absence of partitions inside help to lighten the weight of the omnipresent wooden paneling.

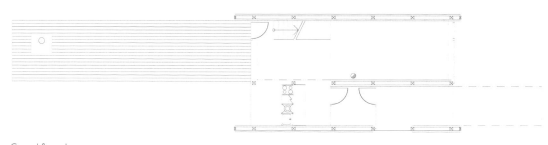

Ground-floor plan

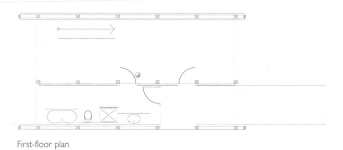

First-floor plan

Photos © Laurent Brandajs, Counson Architectes

POB_62

Counson Architectes   Houffalize, Belgium

POB_62 is the prototype of a prefabricated home. For this project the architect wanted to recover the essence of the western home, and then design a model that because of its abstract appearance and the simplicity of its shapes, can be adapted to other environments and needs. The 665-square-foot POB_62 (plus 155-square-feet of terrace) is based on the repetition of a 50 by 245-inch unit, which can be used to create larger houses without appearing to have modified their basic characteristics. The prototype in the photograph, located in the Belgian region of Ardennes, was designed to accommodate tourists desiring to immerse themselves in the area's natural beauty. With the exception of the base, POB_62 is built entirely from wood. It consists of two sections arranged linearly and joined by a glazed section clad with the same panels that cover the two bodies on the open façades. A layer of alerce wood, laid like scales, covers the roof and opaque façades, while the other two are formed from large French windows. The interior finish is chipboard, with the exception of the central block, which hides the bathroom. This block receives natural light due to its location at the joining point of the two sections that make up the house.

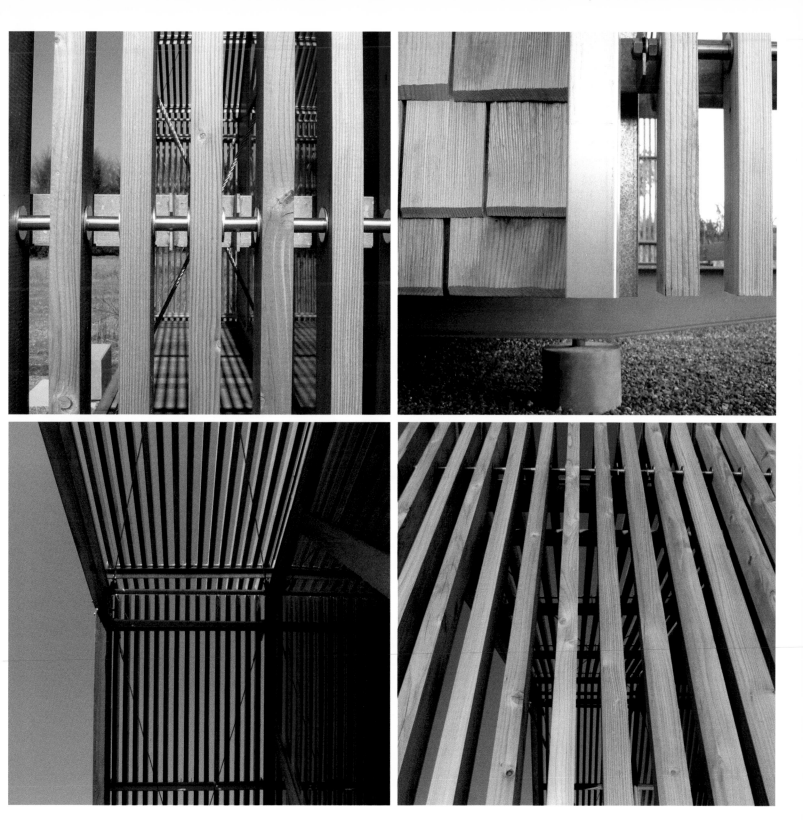

Due to POB_62's nomadic character, the volume, which is easy to assemble and transport, rises from a metal structure that allows it to be installed on different types of terrain.

One of the main characteristics of POB_62 is its optimal use of natural light.

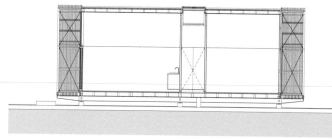

Longitudinal section

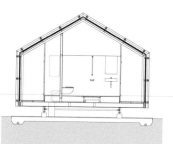

Cross section

The porches, which are protected by a structure of panels, were conceived as a transitional space between the open scenery and the interior of the home.

Photos © Ben Rahn

Bondi Junction Residence

David Boyle Architect   Bondi Junction, Australia

The project of Australian David Boyle reinterpreted the typical semidetached constructions from the early 20th century with a contemporary touch, while maximizing the surface area of this type of house. In order to increase the amount of square footage available to the 945 of the final renovation, the architect raised the roof to the height of the neighboring houses. This allowed him to add a new floor to be used for a bedroom and bathroom. The ground floor was then subject to considerable change, which made better use of the space. The living room and kitchen form an L shape around the courtyard, whose floor and north wall are clad in

ood. At the southeast end of the courtyard and following on from the kitchen is a roofed space, which allows for barbecues in any weather. One of Boyle's aims was to provide his clients with a unique home. With this in mind, the architect incorporated various works of art into the interior design scheme. A sculpture made from scrap wood adorns the living room, while the courtyard has been enhanced by a concrete relief and a colorful mural. Among other details, which not only give the renovation originality but also ingeniously make the most of the space, is the foldable table in the kitchen or the benches in the courtyard.

The bench in the living room constitutes a favorite spot due to the small adjoining garden with its own pond.

The elongated narrow form of the plot led the architect to align the bedroom, bathroom, and study along the same side of the corridor, which also houses the stairs.

The large glass doors that open to the courtyard can be taken out completely to favor ventilation, which is further optimized by the numerous openings in the rest of the house.

In order to minimize the visual barriers, only the change in the flooring marks the boundaries between the kitchen, living room, and courtyard.

The peculiar rounded wall that surrounds the bathroom stands out on the upper floor, whose multicolored mosaic breaks up the continuity of the white.

Longitudinal section

A skylight supported by a copper chimney provides natural light and ventilation in the bathroom, and constitutes a perfect point of reference to locate the house at night.

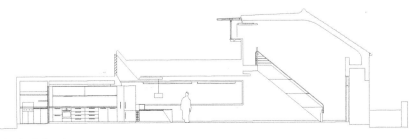

Longitudinal section

Photos © Rob't Hart

Copypaste House

UCX Architects   Alblasserdam, The Netherlands

Alblasserdam, especially know for its proximity to the famous Kinderdijk mills, is a small city in Holland's southern province. The site of Copypaste House sits parallel to one of the numerous dikes that stop the sea from flooding the region, nominated a World Heritage site by UNESCO in 1997. The project consisted in carrying out an extension to a house originally built more than a century ago on a considerably sloping plot. UCX Architects conceived the new 810-square-foot house as an identical copy of the first one, making use of advanced technologies and materials that have appeared since the original creation. Although

the copied structure is almost identical to the original, the two volumes differ from the outside due to the wood and metal cladding chosen by UCX for the new façades and roof, respectively. The house consists of three floors, situated at different levels in one volume or the other but connected by stairs. The two basements are used for storage; the living area and covered space housing the bedrooms are found on the ground floor. In the new volume, the surface area of the ground floor is reduced by half due to the double height of the living room.

The living room, located in the
new volume, pays homage to the
landscape of old mills, as a large
window affords views of the
unending plain where these
constructions are situated.

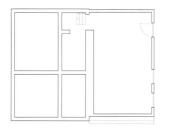

Ground floor

First floor

Second floor

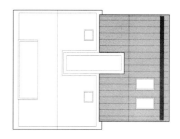

Roof floor

Elevations

Elevations

Longitudinal section

Perspectives

Photos © María Masieri/Photo Nider

Holiday Home in the Forest

Besonías Almeida Kruk   Mar Azul, Argentina

Mar Azul an area of sand dunes and conifer forests on the coast near Buenos Aires, has developed as a tourist destination for many Argentineans. Among these are the owners of this house, who are members of the studio of architects commissioned with this project. Due to the absence of a client to determine the conditions of the construction and the seasonal use of the house, the architects were able to experiment with both functional aspects and aesthetic and constructive solutions. The project's objectives were to minimize the house's impact on its environment, work within a restricted budget, and minimize the amount of maintenance needed.

The house was designed as a first volume—a round glass and concrete prism—and a wooden tower, hidden in the trees, used for all complementary functions. The main 810-square-foot house, was developed from two large slabs of concrete containing two different areas: one glazed and surrounded by a large terrace, and the other, more protected, housing the bedrooms, bathroom, and kitchen. This simple and economic constructive solution, with no need for thermal insulation, was viable due to the microclimate of this seaside forest, and the intention of uing the house only during the warmer months of the year.

The texture and color of the roof's concrete, as well as the large panes of glass in the communal area, integrate the main volume with the forested surroundings.

Because the house can be accessed via any of the sliding doors of the living room, the communal space can be adapted to the needs of the moment.

The furniture, designed especially for this project, was made from Canadian pine wood recycled from boxes used to pack engines.

The interior and exterior concrete was sandpapered by hand, reducing considerably the costs of the project and its time of completion.

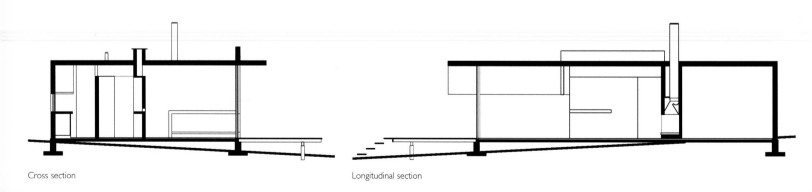

Cross section

Longitudinal section

To optimize the natural light an opening was positioned at the central area of the house, creating a light effect that changes throughout the course of the day.

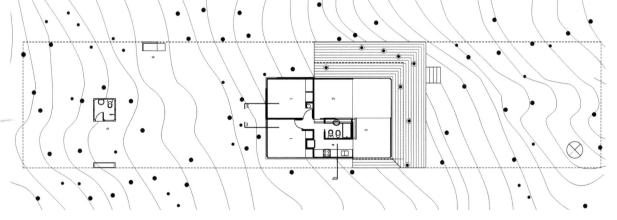

Site plan

Photos © Hannes Henz

Renovation by a Lake

Wespi & De Meuron Architekten Scaiano, Switzerland

This 755-square-foot summerhouse is situated on the outskirts of a small alpine village on the banks of the Swiss-Italian Lake Maggiore. The plot affords amazing views of the lake and surrounding mountains to the northeast, and sits alongside the latest Scaiano houses, whose rich architectural heritage has been well preserved. Due to the location on the border, the architects decided to transform the original house, a simple stone building typical of the area, into a section of habitable wall. After much insistence and discussion of the town's strict preservation regulations, they managed to obtain the authorization to change the gable roof to

a flat one. Maintaining the stone walls intact was another indispensable condition to give the construction the aspect of a wall. Likewise, the original openings were preserved, with slight changes to their dimensions in some cases. The plot's inclination distributed the building on different levels, joined by multiple flights of small staircases. The communal areas are located on the top floor, which houses the access to the home, while the bedrooms and office occupy the other two floors. Because of the limited area of construction, a space was dug from the plot for the bathroom to avoid altering the original structure.

Renovation by a Lake 137

A careful restoration process was carried out on the walls, which included the addition of a buttress to reinforce the northeast wall.

The windows were arranged alternatively flush with or set back from the outside wall, creating an interesting pattern on the façades.

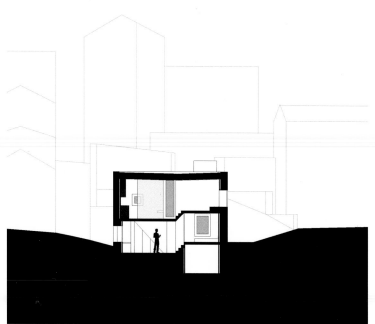

Longitudinal section

Cross section

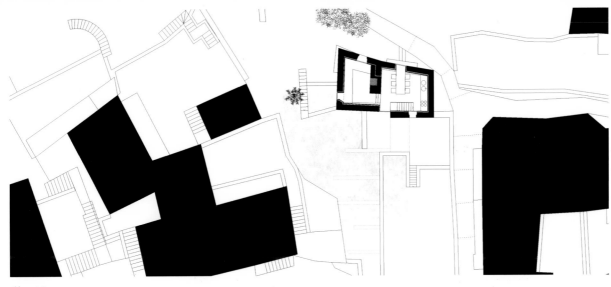

Ground floor

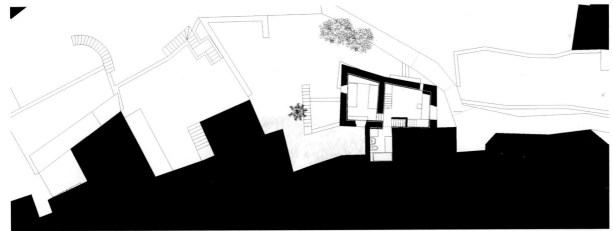

First floor

Inside, the neutrality of the gray flooring, walls, and roofing gives center stage to the scenery and the light, which penetrate through the openings dispersed around the façades.

The surface area of the lower floor is notably smaller than that of the upper ones due to the changing level of the plot.

The access zone of the house has been reorganized to create an outdoor space that connects the construction with the street.

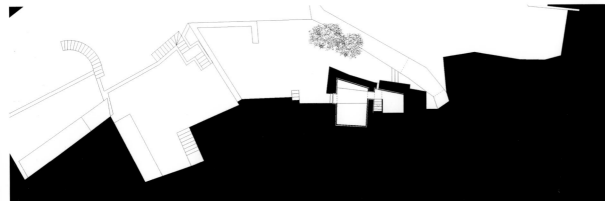

Second floor

Photos © Masao Nishikawa Photography Studio

Unagi 001

Chiba Manabu Architects Tokyo, Japan

Unagi 001 is the first built of three residential prototypes under the Tokyo House program. The three models are based on the most common plot typology: *kado* (corner), *hata* (flag), and *unagi* (eel). The aim of Tokyo House is to reduce construction costs and time through a carefully studied design rather than industrialized construction. The 540-square-foot Unagi prototype is based on the alternation between closed and open: two boxes located at different levels provide intimacy, while the rest of the house is an open, multipurpose space that can be adapted to the specific needs of the occupants. In the case of Unagi 001, the bathroom and soundproof music studio are located in the ground-floor box, while the upper-floor box houses the bedroom. The open spaces on the ground and middle floor are used for the kitchen/dining area and living room, respectively. With the exception of the two boxes, the home is open to the adjacent alleyway, shared with the neighbors as an outdoor space.

The building, sitting on a site of just 385-square-feet, has been constructed of wood and steel, which are also dominant materials inside.

The dividing walls are covered from floor to ceiling with shelving, where the two boxes, furniture, and stairs are inserted.

The living room and bedroom
recieve natural light from the
generous openings on the south
façade, as well as from the
skylight built into the roof.

The arrangement of the two
boxes at different heights and on
opposing façades multiplies the
feeling of size inside the home.

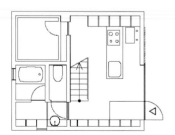

Ground floor

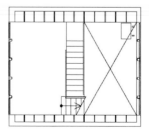

First floor

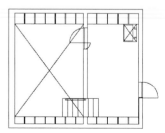

Second floor

Given the absence of doors, the elevated position of the bedroom guarantees the privacy of its occupants.

The bedroom opens onto the living space by way of a pivoting window situated near a skylight.

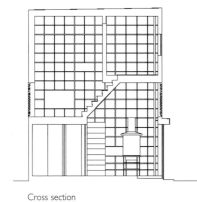

Cross section

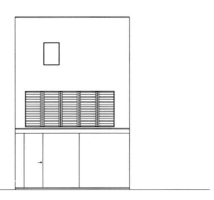

Elevation

Photos © Matevz Paternoster

XXS House

Dekleva Gregoric Arhitekti   Ljubljana, Slovenia

XXS House is located in Krakovo, probably Ljubljana's oldest neighbourhood. In the 15th century it was a small fishing village that provided the nearby monastery with fresh food. Its architectural heritage, including prehistoric and roman remains, is jealously guarded by a legislation which has limited XXS House's surface area to 463-square-feet. Based on the existing dimensions, Dekleva Gregoric designed a summer house for a couple that usually resides in the countryside. The new building, which is north facing, is a rectangular house with an inclined roof in which several openings were made to allow the sun to illuminate the area indirectly during the day. The construction includes a ground floor and two mezzanines with an iron staircase in the middle which hardly takes away from the useful area and allows the sun to penetrate into the room. The ground floor, used as the day area, leads to a small garden through a large sliding window. The living room, kitchen and dining room take up one space, while the bathroom is hidden behind an exposed cement wall in the entrance hall. The mezzanines, flooded with plenty of light thanks to the skylights and the opening in the western façade, take advantage of the house's maximum height, not more than five metres.

The sobriety of the lines and materials means the house's limited space is not overloaded and the iron staircase plays a fundamental role.

The minimalist kitchen opens onto the western façade through a large fixed window and a wooden window shutter.

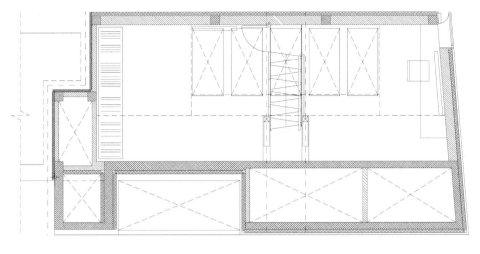

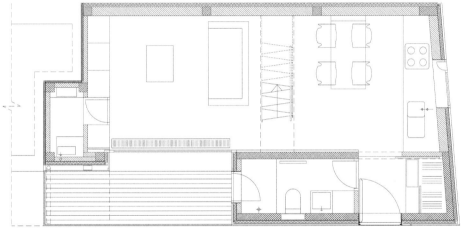

Ground floor and mezzanine

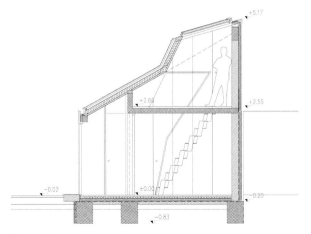

Cross section

From the outside, XXS House is seen as an almost solid block, with the north façade and the roof entirely covered in fibrocement panels. On the inside, however, the opposite effect has been created by the optimum use of natural light.

The roof's considerable incline has reduced the top floor, the bedroom, to a mezzanine with a sloping ceiling.

Photos © Hirotaka Satoh

K-Box

Hirotaka Satoh   Tokyo, Japan

Surrounded on three sides by other low buildings, K-Box sits on a narrow plot in an overpopulated residential area of Tokyo. Despite the lack of available surface area, the architectural project had to adapt to the needs of a five-person family, providing privacy and also a social space, such as a terrace. The design was based on two elongated volumes arranged on either side of a central courtyard. Both the front door and the stairs, which connect the two floors of the house, are located in this outdoorarea to avoid wasting valuable square feet. The three ground-floor bedrooms are aligned along one side of the courtyard and have their own

access via sliding glass doors. This gives privacy as well as inviting the occupants to meet in the central courtyard, symbolic of the family ties. This alternation between dependence and independence is constant throughout the home. The communal area, a single room that encompasses the living room, dining room, and kitchen, is situated on the first floor in order to receive more natural light. This living space connects, via a walkway, with the terrace, which is hidden from view by a lattice on the other side of the courtyard.

To maximize the natural light that reaches the ground floor and courtyard, the height of one of the two volumes, whose roof was used as a terrace, was limited.

The lattice and high concrete walls guarantee the privacy of the occupants of this house, whose neighbors are in close proximity.

In the living area on the upper floor, the kitchen is hidden behind a foldable door.

In this volume the slope of the roof allowed a large part of the perimeter to be finished with a transom to make the most of the hours of sunshine.

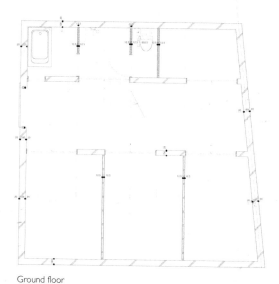

Ground floor

First floor

Photos © Ulf Celander

Summerhouse by the Sea

Windgårdh Arkitektkontor Tjuvkil, Sweden

This small summerhouse is situated on a plot that is only accessible by sea, 50 miles to the north of Gothenburg. Its unique position and the amazing views it affords to the west made the project stand out from the start. Due to the difficulty of transporting the construction materials to the site, the architects decided on a simple wooden house raised above the ground via a platform of the same material. Because of the strict town planning regulations in the area, the surface area of the house could not exceed 855-square-feet, to which 108-square-feet were added in the form of a small guesthouse. The entire volume is covered in

Canadian cedar wood, which was left untreated so that the course of time it would integrate with the rocky surroundings. The design is distributed across a ground floor and two mezzanines, installed at the east and west end of the house. The ground floor, with direct access to the large terrace from all of the façades, accommodates the living area and a bathroom, while the mezzanines are reserved for the bedrooms. The seaside location determined the style of the interior, since the light-colored wood of the floor, furniture, and roofing gives the place a marked marine appearance.

The clients commissioned a summerhouse whose maintenance was reduced to a minimum.

The simple structure of the building is directly related to the area's traditional architecture.

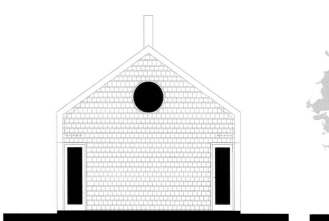

East elevation

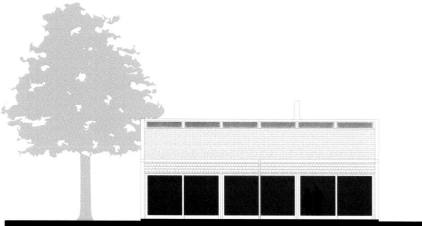

North elevation

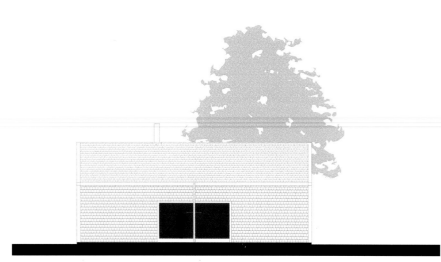

South elevation

West elevation

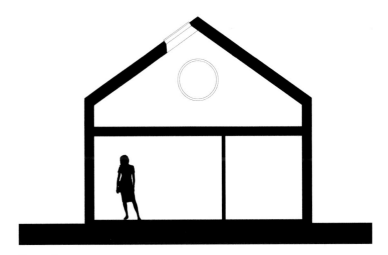

Cross section

Cross section

Due to the almost complete absence of divisions on the ground floor, the two mezzanines have been built on a steel structure.

The mezzanines receive natural light from the various skylights in the roof, as well as from the portholes on the east and west façades.

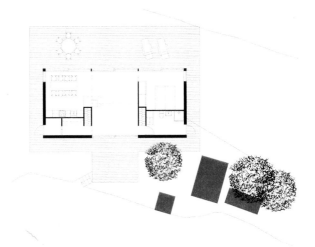

Ground floor

Mezzanine floor

Two Houses in One

Satoshi Okada   Tokyo, Japan

The two volumes of this Two Houses in One project share an elongated site measuring a little over 2,150-square-feet in Okigubo, a densely populated residential neighborhood of Tokyo formed by a chaotic network of alleyways. To the north the site borders a lush garden, while to the south and west it is delimited by dirt roads. Due to the difficulties experienced by young people today when buying their first home, the clients, two generations of the same family, commissioned the architect to build them a house for each family on the site. Given the absence of space, Okada proposed a project based on the concept of

independence in dependence, according to which the families have their own space but share the same building. A zigzag wall irregularly divides the plot into three parts: the central open section to the north and the two south-facing ends. The younger generation occupies the western volume, whose dividing wall leans against the other two parts belonging to the parents. The two homes of 1,035 and 1,080-square-feet, respectively, are functionally independent, and their only nexus is the continuous wall that both joins and separates them. The next floor is occupied in both houses by the kitchen and living room.

This house's peculiar structure draws on the urban labyrinth of small irregular plots that surround the site.

The parents access the house by the main street that runs along the south flank, while the younger generation has an independent entrance in the alleyway on the west side.

North elevation

Longitudinal section

Ground floor

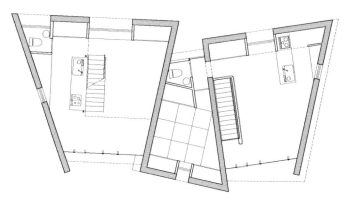

First floor

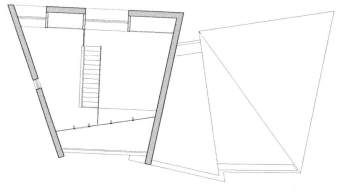

Second floor

In the younger generation's bedroom some surface area was sacrificed to open the space to the outside via a small terrace.

The black exterior of the building, covered in fiber cement panels, contrasts with the interior lighting, where open spaces and straight lines dominate.

The wall that delimits and separates the two homes symbolizes the intergenerational link, one of the fundamental pillars of Japanese society.

Directory

Micro-Compact Home
Horden Cherry Lee Architects &
Lydia Haack, John Höpfner Architekten
34 Bruton Place
London W1J 6NR, United Kingdom
P +44 (0) 20 7495 4119
F +44 (0) 20 7493 7162
info@hcla.co.uk
www.hcla.co.uk

Sunset Cabin
Taylor Smyth Architects
354 Davenport Road, Suite 3B
Toronto, Ontario M5R 1K6 Canada
P +1 416 968 6688
F +1 416 968 7728
info@taylorsmyth.com
www.taylorsmyth.com

Catherine House
Andy Macdonald/Mac-Interactive
Architecture
94 Cooper Street
Surry Hills NSW 2010, Australia
P +61 2 9212 3800
F +61 2 9212 3880
info@mac-interactive.com
www.mac-interactive.com

Kaps House
Caramel Architekten
Schottenfeldgasse 72-2-3
A-1070 Wien, Austria
P +43 1 596 34 90
F +43 1 596 34 90 20
kha@caramel.at
www.caramel.at

Summer Garden Pavilion
Artur Carulla, Rita
Lambert/Eightyseven Architects
27B Canonbury Square London
N1 2 AL England
P +44 (0) 207 3595145
contact@eightyseven.net
www.eightyseven.net

B House
Atelier A5 Architecture and Planning
3-33-12 Daita Setagaya-ku
Tokyo 155-0033, Japan
P/F +81 3 3419 3830
A5@a-a5.com
www.a-a5.com

Lake House
Bercy Chen Studio
1314 Rosewood Avenue, Suite 101
Austin, Texas 78702 United States
P +1 512 481 0092
F +1 512 476 7664
info@bcarc.com
www.bcarc.com

Uncle Fred's Hut
Hertl.Architekten
Zwischenbrücken 4
4400 Steyr, Austria
P +43 7252 46944
F +43 7252 47363
steyr@hertl-architekten.com
www.hertl-architekten.com

C-2 House
Curiosity
2-13-16 Tomigaya, Shibuya-ku,
Tokyo 151-0063, Japan
P +81 03 5452 0095
F +81 03 5454 9691
info@curiosity.jp
www.curiosity.jp

Window House
Kentaro Takeguchi/Alphaville
32 Kamihanada Saiin Ukyoku
Kyoto 615-0007, Japan
P +81 75 312 6951
F +81 75 312 0416
alphavil@a1.ethink.jp
www.a1.ethink.jp/~alphavil

Extension in Dulwich Hill
Nobbs Radford Architects
Level 1 16 Foster Street
Surry Hills NSW 2010, Australia
P +61 2 9281 2722
F +61 2 9281 2733
architects@nobbsradford.com.au
www.nobbsradford.com.au

A House in the Garden
Archteam
Weyrova 3, 547 01 Náchod
Czech Republic
P/F +420 491 422 009
archteam@archteam.cz
www.archteam.cz

POB_62
Counson Architectes
23 rue des Ardoisières
B-6690 Vielsalm, Belgium
P +32 497 42 20 89
bertrandcounson@bluewin.ch
www.counson-architecte.net

Bondi Junction Residence
David Boyle Architect
17 Como Parade
Pretty Beach NSW 2257, Australia
P +61 0419 664 836
davidboylearch@bigpond.com

Copypaste House
UCX Architects
Westerstraat 39b
3016 DG Rotterdam, The Netherlands
P +31 (0) 10 2829 989
F +31 (0) 10 2829 998
office@ucxarchitects.com
www.ucxarchitects.com

Holiday Home in the Forest
Besonías Almeida Kruk Arquitectos Asociados
Buen Viaje 1011, 1° B,
Morón 1708, Buenos Aires, Argentina
P/F +54 11 4489 5424
arqbesonias@yahoo.com.ar
arqkruk@yahoo.com.ar
bakarquitectos.com.ar

Renovation by a Lake
Markus Wespi Jérôme de Meuron Architekten
CH-6578 Caviano, Switzerland
P/F +41 (0) 91 794 17 73
info@wespidemeuron.ch
www.wespidemeuron.ch

Unagi 001
Chiba Manabu Architects
2-5-4-301 Jingmae, Shibuya-ku
Tokyo 150-0001
P +81-3-3796 0777
F +81-3-3796 0788
manabuch@zg7.so-net.ne.jp
www.chibamanabu.com

XXS House
Dekleva Gregoric Arhitekti
Dalmatinova 11
SI-1000 Ljubljana, Slovenia
P +38 614 305 270
F +38 614 305 271
arh@dekleva-gregoric.com
www.dekleva-gregoric.com

K-Box
Hirotaka Satoh
Open Studio NOPE, 2-12-5 Minato-ku,
Tokyo, 108 0073 Japan
P +81 3 5443 0595
F +81 3 5443 0667
webmaster@synapse-net.jp
www.synapse-net.jp

Summerhouse by the Sea
Windgårdh Arkitektkontor
Kungsgatan 10A
SE-411 19 Gothenburg, Sweden
P +46 031 743 70 00
F +46 031 711 98 38
windgardhs@windgardhs.se
www.windgardhs.se

Two Houses in One
Satoshi Okada Architects
16-12-302/303 Tomihisa, Shinjuku
Tokyo, 162-0067 Japan
P +81 3 3355 0646
F +81 3 3355 0658
mail@okada-archi.com
www.okada-archi.com